QUATRAINS 2

Dedicated to
Anne Meehan Malone and Brian Malone

QUATRAINS 2

J. F. Her

ARTHUR H. STOCKWELL LTD
Torrs Park, Ilfracombe, Devon, EX34 8BA
Established 1898
www.ahstockwell.co.uk

British Library Cataloguing-in-Publication Data.
A catalogue record for this book is available
from the British Library.

By the same author:
Streams
Ripples
Once Upon a Time (Cloth Edition)
Once Upon a Time (Paper Edition)
Freedom Dialogue (I)
Freedom Dialogue (II)
Quatrains 1
The Antique Shop

ISBN 978-0-7223-4976-2
Printed in Great Britain by
Arthur H. Stockwell Ltd
Torrs Park   Ilfracombe
Devon EX34 8BA

FRYING AND GRILLING

Prose, in the cooking,
Soaks up fat.

Poesy, well grilled,
Emerges lean.

ASSESSING THE FEEDBACK

When the past keeps babbling,
High time to awake.

When future back answers,
Consider a wee break.

HUMAN FOLLY

For half at least
Ignorance owns up.

With that remaining
Stupidity vehemently denies involvement.

TRENDS

Whims of the moment
Façades avoiding truth

Individual insecurity
In search of a suit.

REACHING OUT

Two ways to reach your subject
When understanding's on welfare:

Work rote till weary
Or dole out humour.

EARLY AND LATE

Said Arrival to Departure:
"We need some time apart!"

Came the reply promptly: "Had I free hand,
I'd wear you on my derrière as art."

THE SELF-RIGHTEOUS

Till the chill of reality dawns
Either side of the sod

Acknowledge truth, not they
Till full stripped amongst their gods.

SUBJECTS APART

Impressing Folly
Advertisers' art:

Bring subject to bosom;
Keep reason at arm's length.

FOUR PAWS TO THE FLOOR

Life in a society
A dream of tomorrow, a concept of yore

Life in an economy
Service on all fours.

TALKING HANDS

Criticism employs but mouth
Plus, on occasions, dancing hands

While change calls for effort
On the heels of plans.

FEELINGS AT A LOOSE END

With time on their hands
Feelings seek out offence.

The mind squanders
At the expense of intelligence.

TREAD SOFTLY ON MY ILLUSIONS

Most are happy to quote others
Where a quote to their speak something adds

But when others mimic follies
Most are wont to get mad.

LAYING CLAIM AND BEARING WITNESS

Time, seeing off both vanquished and victor,
Lays claim to the spoils.

Truth, bowing to all differences,
Bears witness to all wills.

FOLLY'S FAULTY EQUIPMENT

Folly excuses its shortcomings;
Wisdom, not as much as a dot.

The former, noticing the fruits of no awnings,
Believes itself victim of a plot.

FORCE ALWAYS BACKFIRES

Did gun ever solve a problem –
Or for that matter spear?

Valid only two of their claims:
To inflict death or instil fear.

HOT-AIR-LESS BALLOON

Words are helpless
Unsupported by deed

As neutered all systems
Half true to creed.

U TALKING TO I

Who needs to be a media darling
Or mob hero?

What ego doesn't bow to head patted
Or won't schmoozy to message?

BS VERSUS WISDOM

BS, addressing Wisdom,
Asked: "What do you do?"

"Promote growth," replied she,
"After applications of you."

SINCERITY

Can't be taught
Can't learn off by heart

Once introduced to
Can't live apart.

BEYOND RECALL

Upon breaking the barrier of time
Crossed too is the boundary of crime

No boundaries, no barriers remain
Simply eternal loss or gain.

GRASPING THE ILLNESS

Said B to A: "You'd hardly grasp that
Even if handed to you!"

"No!" replied he. "And if you peeped vertically,
You too might notice the logic's left-sided skew."

COMPROMISE

True leaders compromise everything
For the sake of truth.

Those besides compromise everyone
In pursuit of the illusions of youth.

LARGER THAN LIFE

Who feels small in himself
Is forever aware of size

Who needs to make others feel small
Still feels insecure on his hilltop of lies.

REFORMATION

Not consulted
Ill-informed

Abandoned to my will
While to His expected to conform.

AFTERMATH

Belief, blessing
Belief, curse

Supplying hope
In the wake of a hearse.

THEN AND NOW

Different times
Different demands

Different skills
Same hands.

RENDITION

Media go to law
Brandishing half-truth as their right

Twilight waving its fist,
Wishing to assert itself over daylight.

CRIME

Consequences pursue
Systems inept

Energy unharnessed
Society bereft.

SUPPORT BASE

That rung below dung level
Is a lawyer's reserve

And the one just below it
Our elected it serves.

SNOUTY OUTY

Can't sanitise old age
Can't enlighten youth

Can achieve sage
Once tamed is ego's mouth.

LONGEST DAY AND SHORTEST NIGHT

Brevity
Pulsing with truth

Wisdom's heartbeat
Pure thought's fruit.

CRACKING THE WHIP

Thought looks hard at feelings
Then tells them to line up

They, like Jack the terrier,
Ignore, ignore, sit up.

MARKING TIME OR ON THE MARCH

If not by faith,
One lives by appetite

If by truth,
One journeys light.

MAJORITY AND REFORM

About the notion of reform
Majority remains blasé.

It cites in sequence current norms,
Borrowing logic from cliché.

AS LONG AS FOOLS WAVE FLAGS

Not till people play election day
Like politicians play them

Will democracy grow teeth
And sheep learn to bite.

ON STANDBY

God pockets the past
And future He holds in one hand

With the other He stands ready
Should our folly demand.

LEND ME THOSE TOOLS. . . .

Lord! Help me complete Your work of art!
Grant me the wherewithal:

Sincerity of mind
And purity of heart!

SEIZING THE MOMENT

That electorate is averse to taking any lead
Suits elected just grand

And so society's underbelly ever needs Big Mamma
To help its under stand.

ROUNDING UP THE USUAL SUSPECTS

Novelty bats eye
Reason's brought in for questioning

Folly's cut loose
And Wisdom's arrested.

PARTNERS FOR LIFE

Blurring the boundaries
A way of life

For legislator and lawyer
His common-law wife.

OLDEST GAME ON EARTH

Being equal means equalling:
Each supporting his own pack

But Equal and Unequal much prefer
To play piggyback.

TWIN ISSUE OF TRUTH

Ugliness
Why so repellent?

And beauty
So disobedient?

IGNORANCE EXAGGERATES

Genius, like theft,
Makes larger than life

As shortcomings too oft
Defy belief.

LEADING BY REMOTE CONTROL

The more removed the leaders
From the led

The further the engine
From the load.

TENANTS OF TIME

Masters we are not entire
Of our own destiny

Rather, masters by degrees
Of the moment only.

LOYAL TO NO. 1

Prelate like prince
Of the medieval run

Wide open to persuasion
But answerable to none.

SPECIES APART

Each generation
A species apart

The one fails to connect with
What the other would impart.

IMPRESSIONS

Size impresses the small;
Violence, likewise, the weak.

God impresses the humble
As a paradise does the bleak.

IN THIS PRESENT REGIME

When employed,
Can't afford illness

And where unemployed,
Couldn't afford to work.

BLIND SPOT

Knowledge reaches awareness
When accompanied by truth

But where God confers insight
Man tends not to promote.

PERSISTENT DENIAL

Endurable Truth
Difficult to ignore

Recurs and recurs
While awaiting a cure.

DISABLED

Unwilling to reach
Beyond point of view

Unable maybe
That's another point too.

LEASH LENGTH

To teach mob or know-all,
Extend each open-ended credit

Only when ball and chain pinch
Will either acknowledge limit.

WELL WORN BUT STILL GOING

Whether weapons of woe
Or carrot-like cues

Where applied to coerce
Surely failed has your style of verse.

AIMING TO WIN

To overcome an enemy,
Get into his skin:

To get to know yourself,
Subdue the one within.

ATTEMPTING TO POSSESS

Possess we can't beauty
But that doesn't prevent trying

Pluck or fence off we're wont to
And thereafter spend vying.

APPLYING BRAKES TO THOUGHT 1

Thinkers supply channels
To drain chaos

Systems apply strictures
To sustain profits.

HANSIATIC PLOT

Smug makes sleepy
FF fakes clappy

Cubs wake hung-over
Screwed makes sober.

WORLD CLASS

Truth houses wisdom
In a shed

While Folly accommodates itself
Commensurate with grade.

BITING ONE'S TONGUE

While frenzied offence rails,
'Tis charity to disengage.

In empty silence only
Will anger come of age.

INSULATED FROM TRUTH

If you're comfortable in sin,
Then conscience you have overcome.

But if you're comfortable,
Your soul is on the run.

DOCTORING THE INCURABLE

Death can't be bought off
But age can be veneered.

Truth we can doctor
But not the underlying fear.

LYING IN WAIT

Intelligence welcomes criticism
For what it's worth.

Criticism Folly tolerates
Till it sees its way to retaliate.

DAWN OF ENLIGHTENMENT

P. downed a bottle of Wisdom
Over the course of a day

The head was left dizzy;
The mouth, uttering sounds too profound to relay.

ONE TON TO THE OUNCE

Not the wise
Give wisdom place

Rather, tons of folly
To wisdom's ounce.

WASH NOT, WASTE NO SOAP

Who never utters an apology
Runs not the risk of admitting wrong

Of having to start afresh
Or sustaining friendship for too long.

LEASH LENGTH ON TRUST

Tomorrow, that's God's territory.
Today is given in trust.

Yesterday we're wedded to
To better or make worse.

EPIC JOURNEY WITHIN 1

Two millennia en route
Twenty centuries on the march

Forty lifetimes at least
And neither foot the other has passed.

EQUALS ALL

Fools are equals
For all men are

Undoubtedly equal
To themselves.

EXTENDING THE NOTION

Given little notions
Of equality

And folly wastes no time
Asserting superiority.

RAISING THE NOTION

Raise a fool a row
Seat him a moment among the wise

And when he fails to cause a stir,
Wisdom he begins to despise.

HOMESCHOOLING

Raising issue
A crop like none

Where parents fail at virtue,
Succeed they do at sin.

ALIGNING THE COMPASS

Those who make good decisions
Recognise wise advice

Those who don't
Much prefer to play dice.

SINGLE-MINDEDNESS

When a couple of bullies get together,
A colony takes place.

When they start breeding,
An empire happens into shape.

FF MENTALITY

Majority rule
Expressed in code:

I before we
Except when it more benefits me.

TAKER MEETS REFLECTION

Awkward appears a taker
In the presence of "Thank you!"

Within something wiggles
Like relief calling "Due!"

LINES AND CIRCLES

Some learn by pressure
Others, by pain

And they never
Who are motivated by gain.

CONSEQUENCE OF FAITH

Fate awaits
Faith's arrival

The former a consequence
The latter free choice.

DILETTANTE

Objective criticism
Resides at well informed

But not all who indulge pelting
Could provide him with a home.

IMAGE CULTURE

Bellowing 'best selling'
Promoted at length

A catchy title
But patchy content.

LIFESTYLE ILLNESS

Feeding emotions
Guarantees fat

Entertaining them
Accumulates debt.

KEEP OUT!

Whiff –
Something iffy afoot

Pong –
Rapidly approaching truth.

FAIR MEASURE

How much of prejudice is truth?
How much of folly is youth?

What portion of ignorance makes rational?
What measure of clever makes proof?

HANDLING DIEGO

Feelings purr
When patted or tickled pink

And bruise
When made to think.

DEMOCRATIC PLOY

Majority's a fee
Politicians must pay

Once ensconced in position
Own rules only apply.

MANOEUVRE VERSUS FOR REAL

When parties play politics,
Busy they are window-dressing hypocrisy.

When they sing in harmony,
Threatened they feel by democracy.

DINING OUT

Law describes a language
Esoteric true

Raw it defines justice
Save when its Druids prepare the stew.

IS IT A BIRD OR A PLANE?

It enjoys open-ended expenses
Reserves the right to set its own wage

And its solution to all shortfalls:
Look for more of your wage.

SUBSERVING THE STATE

Of all philosophies to date
Consistent is one school:

Legislator and buddies apart,
Citizen reduces to tax mule.

"NO REST FOR THE WICKED"

No arguing with emotions
Be they at work or at play

Even after exhaustion
They've been known to re-enter the fray.

CAREER GUIDANCE

Should you aspire to profession,
Learn to square your thoughts

But if you lean toward broader circulation,
Best to round them off.

TALKING TO SHEP

Should majority raise blood pressure,
Remember, Jack will always think pack,

Apply snout as sole measure,
Growl at displeasure but won't answer Alpha back.

JACK'S RULE BOOK

Dogs don't, as a rule, indulge lies
Mute they find most effective

While wagging the tail
And/or rolling the eyes.

SOARING AND DIVING

Listening reaches the heights of logic
With emotions in flight

And the depths of reasoning
With the brainwashed arguing a point.

MARKING THE BALL

Most expressive the interaction
Between Above and Below

Where either spies opportunity,
Follow-up ain't too slow.

NO PRIVACY ON EARTH

Yesterday knows no privacy
With constant poking about its resting place

Today relates a similar story
With tomorrow forever in its face.

FEELING AND KNOWING

Society's a mule
Possessive of pride

Where the former contents itself feeling,
Each mule prefers knowing it decides.

POLITICS IN MOTION

As the group broadens
Reason dims

Highways nod sideways
When logjammed with whims.

INSULATING COMFORT ZONE

Wisdom
Unlike the cold

Should you insulate against,
You pay for manifold.

TWILIGHT ZONE

In workaday semi-awareness
Preserved have we one flaw of yesterday:

Allowed under prescription is Wisdom
Lest it unleash policy delays.

CAUGHT OFF GUARD

Innocent by law
Till certified

Till overheard by two at least
Arguing with the walking stick.

FINE-TUNING OF STONE

Wonder not when prayer's not heard –
When it appears nothing has stirred

Could be that heart's a bit world-hard
Or the headset a mite blurred.

RATIONALISATION

When in pain
Or suffering we're

Life's pretensions shrink to plane
And presumption turns sincere.

ABOVE THE LAW

The state boldly expresses
Its upholding of democracy

While treating as trespass
Exposé of its hypocrisy.

PETS AND PESTS

Truth on the sofa
Beloved when it snores

But briskly shown the door
When it enters, wearing *eau de curs*.

AMONGST THE JONESES

The more aware of yourself
In public opinion

The shorter the journey
To your core.

DICTATES OF FAITH

Creativity in endeavour
Follows whole-time effort

While in excuses
Accompanies part-time clever.

SLOW LEARNER'S FATE

When your own time hails you,
You've served well as season's bait.

It takes society two generations
To complete a generation's portrait.

MIRROR, MIRROR 2

Everyone agrees with mirror
When applied to everyone else

And to a man we all scream "Error"
When there's a voice attached.

QUEER ADVICE

Said H. S. to seer:
"You sound frightfully queer!"

Came the reply:
"Why then is mouth spouting instead of ear?"

NOT MOTIVATED BY WAGE

Good isn't what one utters
Nor displays

But what one does
Beyond the reach of praise.

PREPARING FOR GROWTH

Inching toward destiny
Arching toward light

Growth is a consequence
Of saying "No!" to self.

BUILDING NOT ON CLAY

Measure sceptically your reputation
On contemporary scales

Tomorrow's opinions far outweigh
Those of today.

MOST CURIOUS FABRIC

The Commandments are so woven
If one is severed, all are frayed

And yet, if but one is serviced,
One by one 'twill all repair.

POSTMODERN POLITICIAN

A media-eying me-me
Midst self-styled somebodies

Whose rants, revelling in echoes,
Don an air of superiority.

LOST IN TRANSLATION

Intention, setting out pure,
Presents on the ground a cure watered down

'Cause loudest voices, vomiting choices,
Receive the crew's undue attention.

"NEW WINE, NEW SKINS"

New reason can't crop
Before mind reaches ripe

So till harvest time hopeful
With old mindset must cope.

SURRENDER OR GROWTH

If truth doesn't challenge,
Then inertia will

But should neither bother you,
You're either a lawyer or criminal.

FISHING THE FUTURE

Ideas are real
If caught in flight

Waiting for them to land
You'll be up all night.

A REALITY, NOT A DEFINITION

Citizen is
From the moment of conception

A citizen of Earth certain
And maybe of Heaven.

EVE'S DISCOVERY

Stepping outside of providence
Carries with it consequences

Stepping out of self
Leaves inconsequence behind.

WHY HIERARCHY UNDERPERFORMS

Title belongs to the position
Not the person

Sad that so many need reminding
While the remainder require enlightening.

LIFE BEYOND BLINKERS

True talent transcends
Prejudice

Much as true justice does
Evidence.

THE SILENT PARTNER

Mob needs to feel it has a say;
Now and then likes invited its opinion

But hates when out of slumber stirred
And asked to make a decision.

EVENTS AND THEIR OWNERS

All life starts small –
Mostly as hope-filled nobodies.

When life has done
History recalls all but nonentities.

ATHEIST AND THEIST

One sees life as summing up
To nothing or achievement.

The other reads deeds
Measuring up to belief.

ONE-WAY TRAFFIC

Life's meaning lies open
To debate

While its borders remain closed
To regret.

FOLLOWING THE LEADER

Spiritual creatures follow
Non-spiritual, too

The former, Creator
The latter, me and you.

EXERCISE EMPOWERS

It takes effort to face the day
But none to stay at home.

Steering requires concentration
But not auto-control.

GETTING TO KNOW ME

If you don't learn to laugh
At yourself,

Then accustom your ears
To others doing so.

FLUORESCENCE

Ahead of His wrath
God always sends His voice.

Before Folly's fluorescence
Comes unrestrained choice.

THE UNHOLY TRINITY

If your destination is contentment,
Strap me, I and myself in the back seat.

To reach happiness though,
Make them get out and walk.

ROBBING AND STEALING

Steal a man's good name
And you strip him naked

Rob a man's illusions
And you've buried him alive.

BUSY AND KNACKY

The giver's a person busy
Taker's laid-back

The former has little time for grievance
The latter, little by knack.

MIND OVER MATTER 1

Majority or mob
Demagogue's cup of tea

Whereupon he has drunk,
Thereon he'll pee.

MIND OVER MATTER 2

Once elected
I'm on the pig's back

I don't mind my twenty stone
And piggy doesn't matter.

CHAIN OF EVENTS

As history expands
And future shrinks

Smaller become the great
With evening out of the links.

ABSENT WITHOUT LEAVE

That we notice our own foibles and faults least
And last if at all

Suggests where mostly we look
And what leastly we're taught.

AVERAGE 1

Seeing what it feels
Hearing what it sees

Swallows by ear,
Believing it has thought.

LEADERSHIP

Size of following
Affords mob its measure of leader

While obedience to conscience
Awards leadership's accolade.

FF SYNDROME

The corrupt
Unwilling to fast

Desire beyond their means
And wish to arrive fast.

FAREWELL TO A PUBLIC MAN

Picking noses, vacant stares
Hearts and thoughts all elsewheres

As orator glorifies
One great teller of lies.

DICTATORSHIP VERSUS DEMOCRACY

Pay with your life
For stating the truth

Rewarded for life
For lying under oath.

HEREDITARY UNTRUTH

Nobility means nothing to the lowly
But the trappings thereof do appeal

'Tis much of a muchness to His Lordship
'Cause he knows full well 'tis unreal.

GREY COMPENSATION

All's not negative with ageing.
One plus there is remaining:

Sense catches up and overtakes you
After half a lifetime behind straining.

REBEL BY NATURE

Whether led or misleading
Emotions will complain

Like the loser, drunk or sober,
Ever in search of blame.

SUSPICIOUS OF STRANGE 1

The village exists comfortably
Without blow-ins

And so the village ends
More or less where it begins.

SUSPICIOUS OF STRANGE 2

No blow-ins
No town, no city

Just feudal lords
And pastures pretty.

SUSPICIOUS OF STRANGE 3

Bright lights and buzz
Alive the inner city

Soulless the sprawl
A blight this cesspit sickly.

DISHONESTY OGLING

Human approval
Forever makes eyes

Like the house of ill repute
There sincerity avoids.

LINES AND CURVES

Without a rule
Low's the probability of a straight line

A faulty one facilitates glitch or bend
No matter how steady the hand.

REASON TO FEAR

One thought per second
Brain in top gear

If that's stretch capacity,
Oh dear! Oh dear!

FEELING SMALL

They need titles
Who feel small within

They lead by dictate
Who have to cheat to win.

TOLERANCE IN SEARCH OF CHOICE

Tolerance enjoys monopoly
Till introduced to choice

I tolerate me
'Cause we're both part of the one slice.

TRUE AND PURE

Reason true
Sensitive to emotions

Emotions pure
Immune to reason.

GO EASY ON THE MESSENGER

If responsible for my existence,
My apologies to the world

But don't hold it against my poor existence
Its role to my shortcomings as herald.

LEAVE REST IN PEACE

Speak no eulogy!
Allow no speech!

If there's an ounce of sincerity present,
Don't cause the deceased to screech.

DEAREST CREDIT

Life amounts to, at most,
A period of grace.

Freewill enables, at least,
Misuse.

PREJUDICE

As with all issues primate,
Prejudice requires parents.

Though sired by pride aberrant
Gestates in ignorance.

INVERTEBRATE

Life's but a moment of awareness
Within weakness encased.

In the absence of wisdom
Passion colonises and reason's displaced.

NO SANITISING OF SIN

Amend we can today
What yesterday has left behind

But not edit history
By fabricating lies.

NO F IN LEADERSHIP

The typical politician
Can be accused of anything

But, in fairness, not found guilty
Of leadership.

LOYALIST BREAKING WIND

Pretensions, pretensions
Stirring a fuss

One person's illusions
Make another's cross.

LOO SCROLL FULFILLING ROLE

All's media savvy
Plus politically correct

Where the corrupt are beholden
To the morally inept.

$U \leq 0$

You look up to somebody only
When you've stopped growing

And down upon
When you're beyond knowing.

PRISON VERSUS HELL

Conservatism
A vista of paradise from the bars of my space

Liberalism
A sprawling cesspit forever in my face.

LOTUS-LAND

Who keeps sedating awareness
Never wakes up

Who keeps denying truth
Never faces up.

COMMANDER-IN-CHIEF

A true leader masters
Not just vessel and crew

But the tides and turmoils also
Of his own seas.

LIFE PEAKS AT OPINION

Life at opinion
Pure fantasy at work

Life post-opinion
Awakens to truth.

WITHIN ONE'S MEANS

Simplicity, sustainable,
Can meet its costs

Complexity, over-borrowed,
Operates at a loss.

POSITIVE THINKING

In the course of your day
Who enters your head

Greet with a blessing
Living or dead.

LOVE 1

What we love
We know

What we're in love with
Will either stunt or cause to grow.

48

LOVE 2

What we love
We empower

What we're in love with
In due course exposes us to sour.

SHELF LIFE AND HALF-LIFE

The amount of yesterday
Buried and forgotten

Defines friendship's shelf life
And its rate to rotten.

GOD LIKES AN INCH OF ELBOW ROOM

Do your best
Then leave the rest to God

Vying to be number one,
Ambitions lead in wasting time.

DISHONESTY'S HOME

Dishonesty prefers camouflage
To reform

And for reasons related
Majority refers to itself as norm.

LAST OUTPOST OF CIVILISATION

As long as one rule restraining
Still holds sway on Earth

Till rid of it
Liberalism won't abate.

LIKE WITH LIKE

Fools compete
With greater fools

Genius competes too
But only with self.

FANTASY IN FLIGHT

Dreams proffer hope
While still airborne

But too often upon landing
Prompt us to flight.

CRUISING AND TOP SPEED

Systems run smoother
With the least amount of thinkers

Spurs to industry
The greatest amount of blinkers.

RAW REALITY

Thinking of truth
Deprives of comfort

Comfort pursuit
Makes truth carry the cross.

MATURATION POSTPONED

Home fails
Where not even one virtue prevails

Where parents await approval
From adolescent wills.

OBEDIENCE TO EGO

Regardless the rule
Or status quo

Within won't contain liberal
Because boundary spells foe.

REACHING AND TOUCHING

Literature entertains
But fails to reach

As truth approaches audience,
It induces itch.

AT HOME ON THE OPEN ROAD

Boundaries prove burdensome –
An unnecessary load

Liberal, like nomad,
Prefers no fixed abode.

CAUSE AND EFFECT 2

Who thinks in terms of money
His thoughts are sold and bought

Whose thinking tends toward power
In darkness it was wrought.

STOOPED BY BIRTH

Those needy of political patronage
To help them stand erect

Have no more faith in Providence
Than belief in fair play or square effort.

QUALITY CONTROL

Each mentality,
Every frame of mind,

Undergoes sieving and sorting
Through Time's sifting hands.

CIOTÓG

Class isn't all simply above and below.
Doesn't life spout *ainniseoir* and *ciotóg*?

Amongst siblings, not to mention committee,
Won't you find the half-saint to five rogues?

DEASÓG

Class doesn't just interface at snobbery.
'Tis also what people know.

Amongst forest and shrubbery,
'Twould be *God help us* if all were to uniformly grow.

REAL TIME

In creative endeavour
Not all's simple, plain-sailing clever.

The last minute amounts to
At least half of the journey.

RETURN OF LOST RELATIVES

Ageing brings with it
Its party of fun

Awarenesses everyone else had long since met
One by one introduce themselves as kin.

LINGO OF THE INERTIAL 1

Criticism has a lifespan
But too often no accompanying scheme.

On hearing its echo's echo
High time to heave-ho.

LINGO OF THE INERTIAL 2

You can rely on electorates
To whinge and scorn

And come polling day
To revert to form.

POLITICS AND POLICY

Honesty errs
Mostly by default

Dishonesty
By design.

ADDICTION AGAIN

Once espoused
There's no divorce

To beyond the grave
You'll feel its force.

DEMOCRACY

Much encouraged
On Planet Worth

Provided it causes no upset
To promoter's wealth.

THE RISE AND FALL

Nothing worth having
Is ever light

Nor of lasting value
If not gotten right.

BEYOND ONE'S MEANS

Conquests are things
Possessed of appeal

But to possess them
Be prepared to steal.

LUKE'S MINDSET

Smug Lukewarm
Homes in on his nest.

In self-preservation solely
Will Luke effort invest.

LIMITS OF INTEGRATION

Real learning likens coming home
But delayed, arriving a mite late,

And it brings with it the feel . . .
Someone else's fate.

MASTERY AND CONQUEST

Mastery and conquest
Each holds only one point of view

To rise above –
To subdue.

OUT OF MY WAY!

Where unwilling to swerve
About a crying need

There not prepared to serve
And thus unfit to lead.

QUIT BUGGING ME!

Challenge to shortcomings
We boldly resist.

To those we warm most
Who rock us to sleep.

CERTAIN SURE

Groupthink knows
It's got truth boxed in

'Cause its cogs have been dervish-like whirling
And all have arrived at the same 'pinion.

BLISS VERSUS TORMENT

Happiest they
The most unaware

While most unhappy they, the half aware
Of their own awareness.

DEMOCRACY'S LOAD

Upper class
Misnomer by pride

Lower's issue
Well heeled.

DEMOCRACY'S MULE

Middle class
Climber by creed

A mule
Aspiring to steed.

DESCENDING AND ASCENDING

A dog, till he gets to know his place,
Will try and try to put you down.

As you get to know sincerity,
You long to measure up.

NOTICING GOBVIOUS

The fool recognises genius
Only when announced

And himself sorely
When by mimic pronounced.

CHANGE

Upon the agenda
Scribbled below the main text

Longest surviving footnote
Addressed to the meeting after next.

COMMANDED TO LOVE

What we love
We obey.

When we don't,
Self has got in the way.

FREEDOM TO DISOBEY

Though a decision,
Love isn't a choice . . .

Rather, the freedom to embrace truth
As opposed to advancing vice.

WANTED ALIVE

Sought since time began
The happy heart eludes all snares

Visits babes at play
And humble men.

THE ECONOMIC MIRACLE 1

Majority busies itself
Feeding greed and habit

While dizzying itself
Providing for illusion and retirement.

TIME ENDEAVOURS TO ENCOMPASS 1

Chaos, homeless
Debris upon the winds cast

Order, a place name
In progress, a nest.

TIME ENDEAVOURS TO ENCOMPASS 2

Chaos more
Order less

Seek order will
The smaller space.

TIME ENDEAVOURS TO ENCOMPASS 3

Chaos, though named,
No face as yet exists.

Evidence suggests
Sketches of order in progress.

EFFORT WASTED

If not in the mind of God,
That is, not part of His plan,

Then regardless how long its legs
Short indeed its span.

AFTER AFTER

After the spoil
Comes rearrangement of rules

Old yoke for old mule;
New mansions for new royals.

ROUND THREE

Germany once again
Is poised to swallow

But where the godless lead
A dark age will follow.

CHOSEN OR CHOOSING

Those who inhabit their emotions
Reside mostly in fears

Whose emotions pay rent
He mostly chooses the ones he wears.

EU 1

In progress
A German hegemony

Uniformity
Exterminating variety.

EU 2

Liberals' dominion
A civilisation on the brink

You're at liberty to express an opinion
But informed as to how you should think.

MOB CONTROL

Be it in strife
Or in time of calm

All systems of government amount to
Variations on a theme.

COMING TO TERMS WITH THE WILL

When the head won't carry it,
Build a framework that will

But upon discovering it can't
We awaken at least to what we weren't willed.

STYLE AND SUBSTANCE

Fashion-dependent scribbling
Like couture in its prime

Impress it does its following
But fails outright the test of time.

ADVANCING AND RETREATING

Thinkers retreat to the real battlefront
Where thickest the traffic in thought

While polished fools and their faces
Seek advancement to public places.

UNIFICATION THEORY

Come hang-ups or hiccups
At currency practice meets theory

Here too all generations see eye to eye
And all cultures agree.

DEALING WITH CHANGE

While life in the Garden felt cosy
The pair dealt with instincts at ease

As the winds there grew chilly
Acute became their sense of appease.

ADVANCING ONESELF

If looking for truth,
Can't afford to remain quiet

But if for approval,
Keep muzzle by snout.

DEMOCRACY 2012

A system of servitude
Albeit revenue bar-coded

The higher the tax mule's effort,
The greater its load.

PARTY BREW

Party politicians are what we gather
From our own choice of fruit.

Ridicule we resort to
When we sip their juice.

FAMILIAR ELECTION PROMISES

Gratuitous that generosity
At someone else's cost

And rarest that justice
Where power is lost.

IN THE FULLNESS OF TIME

In God's time
On time

Earlier or later
You've sidestepped perfect.

WORD POWER

Words are most effective
In that dialogue with self

And most destructive
When employed to propel truth.

GLORIA MUNDI

Aim your efforts at the present
And you'll quickly be forgotten.

Direct your talents at tomorrow
And their memory may slightly outlive the coffin.

CAN AND CAN'T

When Can beckons,
We drift or journey forth.

Where Can't stands pat,
We grow or hold court.

DELAYED TILL FURTHER NOTICE

The obvious
Highlighting won't enhance

Though irritate 'twill Inertia
Progress 'twon't advance.

FAITH AND BELIEF

Life's a noisy deception
Regardless of belief

Death, conditional on faith,
Presumes relief.

EARTH'S JUDGMENT

When you screw a friend,
One of that true breed rare

In spite of what you think you've gained
Your portrait depicts you bare.

LOSER BORN

Anger, though never rational,
Mustn't always be unjustified

But whatever its qualification
Fails even when pacified.

SHOTGUN WEDDING

Intelligence and lies
Where forced to equate

Stand either side of inequality
Like early and late.

THE ONLY WAY OUT IS UP

Running from our limitations,
We long for a place of rest

Fleeing extreme heat
Of a skin we can't divest.

POSTPONING REALITY

Truth denied
Wards off awhile a threat

What fails to penetrate the head
Won't permeate the heart.

FLAG-WAVER

Truer to type than oath
Brayer more than thinker

Led from cradle, mule from stable
Bound to bit and blinker.

SPIRIT AND FLESH

For the unwilling
Truth is always out of phase

For the unable
Always out of reach.

FUNNEL VISION

When you patronise,
Two things elude you:

The whole person
And your own frailty.

WEEDS INVADE CORN

Distractions teasing
Mob the vacant head:

Returning to haunt,
Youth wasted dilutes my yield.

FAMILY AND FRIENDS

Said Dan to his wife, Joanne:
"I've finally figured it out."

"Friends are God's compensation
For family."

DIVINE CALLING

Besserwisser acknowledges
Everyone else knows less.

What evades his antennae though:
Everyone's taking the piss.

VERTICAL AND HORIZONTAL

Getting head round the problem,
Cliff face nods upwards

Solving the problem
Seas beckon to sails.

TAKING GENEROSITY BY THE THROAT

Current perspectives
Reflect current light

When allowed to park up for free,
Come to behave as given a right.

DEMOCRACIES AND DEFINITIONS

No platform
No rights

Entitled by definition
But defined by price.

LEAN AND HUNGRY YET

That Shakespeare is still hailed,
Most refer it to his genius.

Were he here, he'd surely say:
"It worrieth me their even greater meanness."

INSECURITY SEEKS NUMBERS

Two weaknesses
Ensure a fall

One strength
Buoys up a crumbling wall.

FAMILIAR AND UNFAMILIAR

Slave longs for freedom
But in unfamiliar poorly survives

Knave wrongs not for kingdom
And in familiar can't thrive.

NATURE SURCHARGING

When change detours
Or dilly-dallies,

Normality exaggerates
Our inner chaos.

SCOIL ÉIRE AS BÉARLA

Here at New Liberal Ireland
We aim to lecture the world

By erasing our culture –
Succeeding where Tudor and Cromwell failed.

RECIPROCALS

Denial
Honesty's inverse

Where one fattens
The other starves.

AWOL 2

When emotions are enlisted
To lead thinking

Is there cause for wonder
When poor reason does a runner?

MASTER ROAD-BUILDERS

Legislation
The liberals' road map

Enables them plot
Any route to no wrong.

LONG-TERM LOTTERY

Living by opinion
No investment, no cost

Life by faith
A lifelong investment on trust.

GROUPTHINK 2018

Patrols the state
In search of dissent

Reason's on remand
For repeat disobedience.

LITRA TOUR

A wonder-filled thing literature!
It transports to anywhere,

Returning you enriched and more aware
To the beloved rocking chair.

CHASING THE WIND

Not easy to educate a complex
Hard to access a ghost address

Inferior/superior for example
One dim phantom plaguing its half-brother.

BIRTH VERSUS GROWTH

No one enters life alone.
Everyone's accompanied by sentry.

Not so with growth –
No one but yourself on duty.

ADMINISTERING FAITH

The more ornate the temple
Poorer the faith.

The heavier the basket collection
Mightier the prelate.

TIME MANAGEMENT

Know-all skirts by Clever
Along the bypass

He can't afford to waste time
Where he knows he won't impress.

PARADISE REGAINED

Liberals, like flies,
Sqworm about decay

Upon they feast
Within their eggs they lay.

TAX MULE COMPLAINS

Wearisome, the weight of a burden.
That of a pleasure, light.

"Can you see", said minister to mule,
"The difference between heavy and light?"

POLITICAL CORRECTNESS

Where cesspool self-protects
By staging attacked –

If a carrier of the illness,
You're legally bound to infect.

TAKING A LEAF FROM HER BOOK

Nature takes her time
Doing the wrapping

While avoiding poisoning herself
At the scrapping.

YEAST WITHIN, NOT OUTSIDE

Greatness doesn't mean standing above
Beckoning upward

Rather, there among,
Helping the batch to rise.

GETTING UP OR ROLLING OVER

Who sets out for truth
Arrives naked.

Who stays put dreams about free
While advancing in wicked.

OVERSTEPPING

No law proscribes admiring beauty
Neither in Heaven nor on Earth

But all laws we transgress
In our drive to possess.

SUCKING UP TO SOCIETY

When we seek approval,
Too sure we're not of ourselves.

Who seeks society's,
That's a sheep looking to befriend a wolf.

"TO EVERY COW HER CALF"

To each right
Its obligation

To every freedom
Its responsibility.

TAKING RESPONSIBILITY, TAKING THE LEAD

Those behind
Rely on my lead

When I lose focus,
They pay in years.

CREDIT WHERE DUE

God rewards effort
Sincere only

Success He reserves for Himself –
With His cup of tea.

UPPER ECHELONS

Snobbery
Uppermost rung of self-deception

Robbery
Of another's dignity.

CREATURES OF THE NIGHT

When exposed to daylight
Lies gasp for dear life

They long for nightfall –
A return to mischief.

TERMS AND CONDITIONS

Atop the food chain creditors abound
Beneath them, worms of various forms

Above the storm clouds creditors drone
Humming in mantra their terms.

RACING TO CATCH YESTERDAY

Human life
Once a garden of delights

Now an ongoing journey
Between delayed flights.

IN THE VOID

Within nature
But as if outside

Between instinct and reason
Emotions joyride.

ALIVE AND WELL AND DECOMPOSING

That which serves
Has purpose

What serves self only
Has already begun to decompose.

THE OLDEST PROFESSION OF FAITH

What we believe
That's how we live

What we profess leaves a wee gap
But wide enough for self-deceive.

ÉIRE'S OLD FAITH VERSUS NEW

Where behaviour of the few condemns the many
There all counts as straw unless equatable to money

Where behaviour of the many condemns the few
There all counts as kosher unless true.

LIBERALISM

Expands and expands
Across all boundaries

Ever in search of
Lowest common denominators.

TINY VERSUS VAST

Tiny knowledge
Scathing in judgment

Happily unaware
Of its vast ignorance.

HOLDING UP THE SHOW

Youth knows well
It's got the answers

If only all besides
Could be deemed cancers.

"KNOW THYSELF"

He travels further
Who keeps improving

Who doesn't linger
At his illusions.

HE AND SHE

He and she
Ply different agendas

Both concur
Round about pretendas.

POLITICS AND PERVERSION

If integrity makes it to priesthood,
There the miracle ends.

For beyond and above reside hand in glove
And to progress requires competence at corrupting.

SUCCEEDING VERSUS LEADING

To succeed in a democracy
Knead the commonest denominators

To lead in a democracy
Feed the greater appetites.

CACOPHONY

Sign of our times
Nothing rhymes

Even level 5s feel cocksure enough
To challenge level 9s.

URGE TO ITCH

Truth is a flea
In Dishonesty's fur

No rest for poor creature
Till complete the purge.

CRAVING AND CURING

Career draws the insecure
As status appeals to the socially aware

Truth satisfies the enquiring mind
Like honest effort pleases the Lord.

NORM

Collective follies of the crowd
Manifest in how easily it is duped

How much it challenges reason
And the ease with which 'tis hooped.

EXCEPTING THE TREE

Wherever your habitation,
Whatever you may be,

Should you outlive your generation,
You become a foreign body.